Original title:
Life's Big Questions, Answered by Pizza

Copyright © 2025 Creative Arts Management OÜ
All rights reserved.

Author: Helena Marchant
ISBN HARDBACK: 978-1-80566-283-9
ISBN PAPERBACK: 978-1-80566-578-6

**The Taste of Tomorrow**

What's the meaning, is it cheese?
Toppings blend, if you please.
Crusty dreams with sauce so bright,
A slice of hope in every bite.

Pizza spins, like life's great wheel,
Sausage wisdom helps us heal.
In each slice, a thought unfolds,
Tales of future, crust and folds.

## Chew on This

Why do we chase the big delight?
A cheesy world, both day and night.
With pepperoni, life's not bland,
Let bacon guide us, hand in hand.

Craving answers, we do explore,
With each bite, we yearn for more.
Saucy questions, oh what fun,
In the oven, we become one.

**Satisfying Questions**

Is there purpose in a pie?
Both thin and thick crusts justify.
Tomato questions rise and fall,
With garlic knots, we've got it all.

Every slice tells a new tale,
From veggie wonders to the pale.
In the box, our dreams reside,
As cheesy thoughts take us for a ride.

## Mellow Mushroom Mysteries

What's life's secret, crust so round?
With mushrooms lurking, wisdom found.
Saucy antics, playful cheer,
A laugh in every bite we steer.

Gather 'round, with friends so dear,
Slice by slice, we all revere.
In this doughy realm, we dwell,
The mysteries bake, we eat so swell.

**Slices of Wisdom**

What is the secret to joy, they inquire,
Is it money, or fame that they desire?
I smiled and said with a wink, you see,
It's the pepperoni on my slice, oh me!

When faced with choices of crust or topping,
The answer is clear, there's no need for stopping.
Just grab a slice, don't think too hard,
Each bite is a lesson, life's not so marred.

## **Toppings of Truth**

How do we find what truly fulfills?
Some say it's knowledge, others say thrills.
I say it's garlic, and maybe some cheese,
A sprinkle of love brings us to our knees.

What's the meaning of every great quest?
They ponder profound, and I take my rest.
Just add some olives, and don't forget sauce,
Enjoy with a friend, no need to feel lost.

## **Crusty Queries**

Who are we really? What's our big role?
Is it complex theories or a simple goal?
I think it's sharing a warm slice of pie,
While laughing at jokes that make our hearts sigh.

Why is existence so vast and bizarre?
Are we just toppings on some giant star?
Let's relish the crust, the chewy delight,
As we ponder the stars and the pizza tonight.

## The Cheese of Existence

Is there a plan, or are we just fate?
With extra cheese, I just can't contemplate.
I chuckle and munch, it's all in the dough,
When you've got hot slices, you're never alone.

What happens when our time's finally done?
Do we simply vanish, or roll in the fun?
I say we come back as pizza divine,
In the great oven of life, we forever entwine.

**Saucy Sentiments**

Why ponder the stars, my dear friend?
Let's dig into sauce that will never offend.
Toppings our dreams, we pile high,
With each cheesy bite, we learn to fly.

Is it love or just cheese on my plate?
Who needs a partner when crust is so great?
Each slice whispers truths, oh so bizarre,
In the oven of life, we're all a la carte.

## The Slice of Wisdom

A pizza slice holds secrets untold,
In the heat of the oven, wisdom unfolds.
Pepperoni circles, like clocks they remind,
Time's just an illusion when we eat, so unwind!

Do we need a map to show us the way?
Or just a pizza to brighten the day?
Each bite a question, a quest for some fun,
With a side of garlic, pizza's second to none.

## **Unfolding Layers**

Each layer reveals a story so grand,
Like questions in sauce that we just can't bland.
Pineapple's a debate; toppings collide,
But laughter erupts when pizza's our guide.

In the quest for the perfect pie slice,
Philosophy fades, all logic's sacrificed.
Is it fate or just hunger that drives,
In the kingdom of cheese, our joy truly thrives.

## The Crusty Chronicles

Gather 'round folks for tales of the crust,
In flour we trust, and in pepper we must.
Questions like toppings, oh so diverse,
With a crusty conclusion, we'd gladly rehearse.

From deep dish to thin, we ponder and munch,
Is the secret of life hidden in lunch?
Each slice a decision, oh what shall we choose?
As we figure it out, let's just eat and snooze.

**Craving Clarity**

When you're lost in thought or cheese,
A slice can bring you right to ease.
With crusty edges, crisp and warm,
Pepperoni thoughts become the norm.

In every layer, wisdom grows,
Tomato sauce, it surely knows.
Just grab a slice, forget your fears,
Two extra toppings and some cheers!

## The Tasty Truths

What's the secret to a zestful life?
Maybe it's just less work and strife.
With garlic knots on the side to share,
Who needs answers when you have flair?

Beneath the cheese, the truth can hide,
A combo special, our taste buds guide.
Slicing through doubt with every bite,
Happiness served hot, goodnight!

## Oven-Baked Answers

In an oven of dreams, we bake our fate,
Pepper and mushrooms can help translate.
When the heat is on, and questions loom,
The scent of basil sweeps away gloom.

Each slice a story, delicious to feel,
Dough twisted tightly, a cosmic wheel.
From saucy debates to cheesy delight,
A pizza party keeps spirits bright!

**Pies of Purpose**

What's more fulfilling, a pizza pie?
Or pondering 'why' beneath the sky?
With every slice, we take a chance,
Doughy adventures, let's start to dance!

Crusts that carry dreams and schemes,
Funky toppings, beyond our themes.
Bite into bliss, let laughter swell,
In each cheesy corner, all is well!

## Cheesy Conundrums

Why is the sky blue, we often muse?
Grab a slice, let the toppings choose.
Pepperoni or olives, that's the key,
Life's puzzles solved over pizza, you see.

Is it fate or just random chance?
A trip to the pizzeria leads to romance.
Cheese pulls and laughter fill the air,
With each bite, we shed all our care.

## Questions Baked to Perfection

What's the purpose of our daily grind?
A slice of pizza can ease your mind.
Margherita or Hawaiian, what should you pick?
Each crust tells tales that come quick.

Why do we dream, what do they mean?
A deep dish pizza is fit for a queen.
With every bite, ponderings fade,
As cheesy goodness serenades.

## Doughy Dilemmas

Is time a circle or a straight line?
With garlic knots, we're feeling fine.
Each topping reminds us, life is a feast,
From pepper to veggie, joy is released.

What is love, and how does it grow?
Maybe it's shared over doughy dough.
Pan or thin crust, let's debate,
In pizza we trust, it's never too late.

## The Sauce of Understanding

Why do we work, is it for the thrill?
With a slice in hand, let's chill.
Extra sauce, we layer on thick,
Finding answers can be quite a trick.

What's the secret to happiness found?
It's pizza nights, gathered round.
Cheesy and warm, friends by our side,
In savory wonders, we take pride.

## **The Essence of Flavor**

In the oven, dreams collide,
Cheese and crust, a warm confide.
What is joy? It's every slice,
Pizza's warmth, oh so nice.

Here's a question that confounds,
Is pineapple good? Taste it round!
Saucy debates, toppings in tow,
Philosophy? Just grab a dough!

Each pepperoni, a tale to tell,
Is this heaven? Can't you tell?
Cravings answered with each bite,
In a cheesy, savory delight.

So when in doubt, just take a chance,
Let that glorious pizza dance.
For every question, big or small,
A slice of pizza solves them all!

## Cravings and Contemplations

Amidst the toppings, thoughts arise,
What's the meaning behind those fries?
With each crust, a new quest forms,
To find out why my heart it warms.

Is it better thin or thick?
Sauce or cheese? I do the trick.
Should I share, or keep it all?
With a wink, I take the call.

Calzones wondering, 'What's my fate?'
Should I eat or hesitate?
With each bite, contemplations swirl,
The answer's clear: just eat, my girl!

So many toppings, a joyous spree,
Garlic knots, a 'yes' from me!
Questions fade with every chew,
Pizza logic, always true!

**Tasting Truths**

What is the secret to happiness?
It's found in dough, that's no guess.
Cheesy smiles and toppings galore,
Life's puzzles, solved at our core.

Do we ponder too much on fate?
As long as I can eat, it's great!
Doughy wisdom in every slice,
Cravings fulfilled, oh, that's nice!

Is it normal to have this thrill?
With pizza nearby, I always will.
Every bite's a mini quest,
Who needs answers? I'm feeling blessed!

So grab a slice and take a seat,
Let laughter and toppings meet.
In cheesy truths, we shall delight,
Pizza magic, every night!

## **Slices of Insight**

When the world feels heavy, take a slice,
Cheese drips down, oh so nice.
What is love? A topping divine,
In garlic knots, we intertwine.

Questions swirl like dough in air,
What's the secret? It's in the care.
A bite of joy, a crunch of fate,
Is pineapple wrong? Just contemplate.

## Mozzarella Mysteries

What's the meaning behind the crust?
Is it crisp, or simply just must?
In a swirl of sauce, life's answers gleam,
Stretch that cheese, it's more than a dream.

Why do we yearn for cheesy bliss?
It's the pull and stretch we cannot miss.
In every slice, a wisdom bite,
Pizza, my friend, makes wrongs all right.

## Pepperoni Philosophy

To share or not? The age-old plight,
Will my pepperoni bring delight?
What is truth? A savory taste,
With every topping, we interlace.

Why does cheese bridge hearts so wide?
In gooey warmth, we can confide.
Do we need answers? Perhaps a pie,
A slice of comfort, oh my my!

## **Piping Hot Perspectives**

Why is the world round like a pie?
Do toppings sing? Can crusts fly high?
Sitting down, which slice do we pick?
Each bite is deep, just like a trick.

What makes us laugh or even cry?
Maybe it's pepper flakes, oh my!
In every question, each tasty dough,
Is a slice of fun, let's go with the flow.

## Flavorful Futures

In a world where toppings reign,
A slice of joy, no room for pain.
Sausage dreams and pepperoni,
Crusty hopes, never lonely.

Cheesy visions, oh what fun,
With each bite, worries undone.
Mushroom musings, savory schemes,
The future's bright with cheesy beams.

## Harvesting Happiness

In a garden of dough, we sow delight,
With veggies fresh, oh what a sight!
Basil whispers in the breeze,
Tomato sauce brings me to my knees.

A feast among friends, laughter in air,
Every slice shows how much we care.
Pepper flakes sprinkle smiles around,
In this party, joy is found.

**Curing Cravings**

When hunger strikes, hear the call,
A pie awaits, the best cure of all.
Slice by slice, the magic grows,
Each topping chosen, happiness flows.

Garlic knots heal hearts in need,
Calzone comfort, a savory creed.
With every nibble, cravings cease,
Pizza party, it's pure release!

**The Pan of Possibility**

In a pan so deep, dreams overflow,
Infinite toppings, the way to go.
Mix and match in saucy delight,
Each bite a mystery, pure and bright.

From hawaiian bliss to BBQ charm,
Every creation, a tasty alarm.
Embrace the adventure, don't be shy,
Crispy crusts beneath the sky.

## **Layers of Love**

In each slice, a story is spun,
Toppings piled high, oh what fun!
Crusty edges holding it tight,
A cheesy hug that feels just right.

Underneath that bubbly sheen,
Is it fate or just a dream?
Sausage whispers, mushrooms speak,
United we munch, it's bliss we seek.

**Tantalizing Thoughts**

What's the secret for joy in a bite?
A sprinkle of herbs, oh what a delight!
Did aliens land just for a slice?
Or is pizza the meaning of life, so nice?

With every chew, wisdom unfolds,
Are we just toppings, or pure gold?
Pineapple, ham, sweet and sour,
Culinary choices show our power.

## The Oven's Oracle

The oven hums, a sage so wise,
With a golden crust, the truth lies.
Tomato sauce, a saucy muse,
What shall we choose, what shall we choose?

Baked to perfection, every pie,
Answers emerge like steam to the sky.
Will it comfort? Will it share?
In its warmth, we find we care.

## **Pinnacle of Pepperoni**

On a mountain of dough, we playful climb,
Each pepperoni slice, simply sublime.
Is happiness round, or is it square?
Let's grab a slice, and not a care!

With every bite, the truth we taste,
No moment wasted, no time to waste.
So gather around, let laughter blend,
For in this pie, we find a friend.

## Cheese that Questions

What's the meaning, oh so deep?
Is it in the crust, or in the heap?
With every slice, we ponder more,
Is pizza wisdom or just gourmet lore?

Pepperoni stands, a judgment bold,
While mushrooms mumble, secrets untold.
Each topping whispers, gives us a clue,
In cheesy delight, we find the true.

## **Flavors of Thought**

Margherita dreams of purest grace,
While anchovy grumbles, what's my place?
Sausage sings of hearty pride,
In each weird combo, our thoughts abide.

Veggie voices shout, 'Let's explore!'
A slice of garlic bread? Who could ask for more!
In every bite, we gather round,
For answers sprinkled, yet seldom found.

## Edible Epiphanies

A hot slice lands, a moment revealed,
Toppings of truth—our fate appealed.
With crust so chewy, we chew on life,
In every pepper flake, we see our strife.

Pineapple laughter, sweet and sly,
Questions swirl like cheese in the sky.
Artichokes ponder, 'What's our role?'
A doughy inquiry, feeding the soul.

## Pizzas of Purpose

In every oven, a journey unfolds,
A slice of purpose, the universe molds.
Thin crust or thick, which path to take?
In cheesy debates, choices we make.

Toppings collide, like thoughts in our mind,
A canvas of flavor, the answers we find.
With laughter and joy, we rise and we bake,
In the oven of dreams, create what we take.

## Toppings of Time

Why do we wander, stretch so far?
A slice in the oven, beneath a star.
Cheese pulls our heart, like stories we share,
Toppings like dreams, sprinkled with care.

What's the secret to happiness found?
A pizza with friends, laughter abound.
Tomato sauce warmth, it's clearer it seems,
Each bite a reminder of simple, sweet dreams.

Are we lost in the crust, or seeking more crust?
With pepperoni hopes, we place all our trust.
Baking together, we dodge every fear,
In this vast kitchen, there's plenty of cheer.

What's at the end, a slice or a quest?
Foldable goodness, you know what's best.
For under the moon, we laugh and we feast,
One pizza at a time, our worries released.

## Dough and Dreams

In a ball of dough, we roll out our fate,
Stretching for toppings while trying to wait.
Sauce of our wishes, applied just so thick,
Baking our hopes, with love, it's a trick.

What defines our journey, the peak or the pie?
A mix of absurdities, let's give them a try.
With each slice we savor, the flavor stays strong,
Pizza's our answer, and we sing along.

Do we fret over bake times, or simply unwind?\nWith
crusts golden brown, what wisdom we find.
A pinch of salt and a dash of delight,
In pizza we trust; it makes everything right.

What lies at the end? A feast or a flash?
In toppings, we mix and in laughter we clash.
The oven's warm glow, it whispers our names,
With each bite of joy, we set our hearts' aims.

## Slices of Serenity

When troubles arise, and nights seem so long,
A pizza on hand makes the world feel less wrong.
Slicing through chaos with virtues and cheese,
In every bite, we find moments of ease.

What brings us together in times of despair?
A pizza party, with friends everywhere.
Bubbling with laughter, like crust bubbles rise,
Each topping's a treasure, a sweet, cheesy prize.

Do we ponder our purpose while munching on crust?
As pineapples dance, in pizza we trust.
With every fresh slice, we uncover our fate,
In savory dreams, we leisurely wait.

When questions get loud, and answers roam free,
Pizza is wisdom, it's as clear as can be.
With each delightful bite, our hearts softly sway,
In cheesy euphoria, we'll wander, we'll play.

# **Oven-Baked Opinions**

What makes a good life? Extra cheese or more crust?
In dough we believe; it's a matter of trust.
With toppings galore, we argue and jest,
Pizza debates that are truly the best.

Should we stack it or fold it, what's our preference?
In pie's perfect circle, we find our essence.
With olives and peppers, our thoughts intertwine,
Each bite a solution, so tasty, divine.

What's the meaning of flavors that dance on our plates?
A symphony savory, it hardly inflates.
With every thin slice, we savor the chat,
In grease and in giggles, just imagine that!

If pizza could talk, what secrets would spill?
Like how to enjoy, or which toppings to grill?
In this oven of truths, we bake all our dreams,
One slice at a time, we unravel life's schemes.

## Ingredients of Insight

What's the meaning of our days?
Topped with cheese and pepperoni rays.
Each slice, a riddle to unfurl,
With a crust that makes the world twirl.

When in doubt, toss a dough ball high,
Watch it soar and dreams comply.
From deep-dish musings to thin-crust dreams,
In every bite, wisdom gleams.

Sauce stains map the moments true,
Like breadcrumbs leading me to you.
An olive, a mushroom, who's to say?
Each flavor shares a thought today.

So as the oven warms the night,
Grab a slice, hold on tight.
For in this cheesy, baked delight,
Questions fade into delight.

## Baked Epiphanies

Ever wondered where thoughts collide?
On a pizza slice, they take a ride.
With toppings seasoned just right,
Every bite's a spark of insight.

When you ponder, check the crust,
It holds the answers, that's a must.
A sprinkle of humor, a dash of cheese,
Makes discovering truths a breeze.

What are dreams, but toppings asked?
Stuffed with wishes, that's the task.
With each layer, flavors align,
In this round treat, all's divine.

So let the oven do its dance,
In doughy wisdom, take a chance.
Slice away doubts on your plate,
Baked revelations, oh so great!

## A Saucy Life

What's the sauce of your soul?
Is it spicy, tangy, or in control?
Each dollop tells a unique tale,
In the oven, we all prevail.

Chasing dreams, we knead the dough,
In the heat, our passions grow.
With garlic breath and cheesy grins,
Each moment shared, the laughter wins.

From Hawaiian to classic fare,
Pizza shows us life is fair.
With every slice, the secret's clear,
Toppings of joy, love, and cheer.

So raise your slice, toast to the fun,
In this saucy life, we've all won.
With marinara guts and crusty skin,
The joy of pizza's the ultimate sin.

## The Slice That Binds

What brings us close from far and wide?
A pizza shared, it's our joyride.
Each slice cut with laughter's grace,
In the circle, we all find place.

What's the glue that holds us tight?
A cheesy topping that feels just right.
In pepperoni hearts, we confide,
As we share stories, side by side.

Beneath the cheese, deep truths hide,
In every crunch, we cast aside.
Like garlic knots that hold us near,
A slice of life, filled with cheer.

So gather 'round the bubbling tray,
For in each bite, we laugh and play.
With friendship baked in crusty vibes,
The slice that bonds us, it prescribes.

## Tasty Troubles

Why is the sky always so blue?
Does it matter if I wear one shoe?
While pondering my thoughts so deep,
Pizza's here, my worries leap.

What if time is just a slice?
Can you top it with some nice spice?
Questions swirl like dough on a rise,
But cheese and sauce bring sweet surprise.

Am I the pepperoni on this pie?
Or the crust that holds the sky?
With every bite, I chew the doubt,
In melted cheese, I scream and shout.

So as I devour this tasty treat,
I find my troubles can be beat.
Wisdom served with a side of fun,
With pizza on hand, I've already won.

**Savory Solutions**

Is the universe round or a square?
Like pizza, does it matter what's there?
Toppings stacked in a goofy way,
   Shake it off—let's just eat today.

Can laughter truly cure the blues?
Or just extra cheese on a few views?
Saucy debates with friends abound,
   In this crust, joy can be found.

Why do we ponder the meaning of fate?
When all I need is a slice on my plate?
With every bite, it's clear to see,
Pizza solves everything, at least for me.

So if you question what life is about,
   Grab a crust and give a shout.
In cheesy goodness, truths unfold,
In each warm slice, adventure bold.

## Pizza Pie Ponderings

What's the secret to happiness, pray?
Is it found in toppings or doughy play?
Slice by slice, I muse and think,
Perhaps joy's found near hot cheese and drink.

Should I sprinkle love on my pie?
Or is it more about that crazy high?
Grabbing a bite with all my friends,
I find the answer, it never ends.

Could a pizza change the world, you say?
With cheesy dreams, I'd like to stay.
Grease stains on my heart and sleeve,
With every slice, it's hard to believe.

Dough of existence, round and true,
With toppings bright, the fun comes through.
As I ponder pepperoni and glee,
Life's a party—let it be!

## The Crust of Existence

What lies beneath the golden crust?
Is it just flour or something we trust?
Beneath the sauce, the answers hide,
In pepperoni, I take great pride.

Do we rise like dough from the pan?
With every bite, there's a grand plan?
Sharing slices, we laugh and cheer,
Contemplating toppings while downing beer.

Is every pie a slice of fate?
With endless flavors on my plate?
In every crust a story's told,
Of savory dreams, and memories bold.

So let's embrace this cheesy fact,
Pizza brings joy, that's a pact.
In every slice, my heart finds rest,
With pizza in hand, I am truly blessed.

## Doughy Decisions

When choices loom like toppings spread,
A crusty base lies in my head.
Should I go spicy or keep it sweet?
With every bite, I ponder, then eat.

A cheesy question, thick and bright,
I weigh my options with delight.
Pepperoni or pineapple's charm?
A loaded slice won't do me harm.

## Topping the Truth

In the oven of thought, my dreams arise,
I sprinkle wisdom like parmesan skies.
Each layer added is a step we take,
Which flavor's deeper? For goodness' sake!

With every slice, we search and find,
The meaning hidden in cheese and rind.
Is cheese a comfort or a cheesy lie?
These toppings talk when we're feeling shy.

## A Slice of Clarity

In a world full of questions, warm and round,
A simple slice is where truth is found.
What's life about? Ask a hot pie,
Dough rises better when the cheese is spry.

As the sauce simmers, our worries fade,
In every bite, clarity is laid.
With a crispy crust and toppings galore,
I find my answers at the pizza store.

**Pizza Perspectives**

From every angle, a pizza shines,
Life's quirky puzzles wrapped in lines.
Do we share or devour alone?
With each slice served, it feels like home.

The box may fold, but friendships spread,
Toppings unite the words unsaid.
So grab a slice and take a seat,
In cheesy moments, we find our beat.

## Slices of Tomorrow

When the world feels heavy, take a slice,
Cheese and laughter, oh so nice.
Bite your worries, let them go,
Pizza wisdom, in each dough.

As toppings dance on crusty dreams,
Sausage sermons, pepperoni schemes.
With every slice, a question fades,
In cheesy goodness, truth cascades.

So when you ponder where to roam,
Just grab a slice and call it home.
Tomato sauce, a vibrant base,
In every bite, find your own grace.

For on this journey, crust in hand,
Together we'll navigate this land.
In laughter and toppings, we shall see,
The answers were served with extra cheese.

**Dough's Discovery**

In the oven's warmth, secrets rise,
A crust of dreams under the skies.
Kneading thoughts with flour and zest,
In every bite, we find our quest.

Each topping's a tale waiting to tell,
Mushroom wisdom, peppered well.
With slices cut, we share the light,
As dough discovers its wondrous flight.

Questions linger as we feast,
In every crust, a flavor beast.
From marinara to garlic spread,
The universe speaks, on crusts we tread.

So grab a slice, join in the fun,
With each new topping, we've just begun.
In laughter we'll find the answers clear,
As dough discovers what we hold dear.

## Flavors of Existence

Each pizza serves a tale profound,
With every bite, a truth is found.
Basil whispers, cheese does sing,
In every slice, the joy we bring.

Pepperoni circles of fleeting time,
Margherita dreams wrapped in thyme.
Crusty edges, questions arise,
Each flavor hides a sweet surprise.

Are we the toppings on life's pie?
Or the dough that rises, oh so high?
A sprinkle of laughter, a dash of cheer,
In every slice, we conquer fear.

So slice it up, let's celebrate,
With each new flavor, we elevate.
In the pizza party of our days,
Existence served in cheesy ways.

## The Pizza Paradox

In the world of crusts, what do we crave?
Simplicity wrapped in dough so brave.
As toppings clash, and flavors tease,
What's the question? What's the cheese?

Is pineapple sweet or just bizarre?
Does the sauce hold secrets from afar?
Each slice a piece of thought and cheer,
In every mouthful, wisdom's near.

The paradox lies in every bite,
Can pizza make our worries light?
With crust as a compass, we all explore,
In a cheesy universe, who could want more?

So grab that slice, let laughter flow,
In bites profound, our truths will show.
With crust and toppings, we shall see,
In every pizza, life's mystery.

## The Circle of Cheese

In a world so round and bright,
We ponder toppings late at night.
With pepperoni dreams in sight,
A slice reveals the path to light.

But what's the meaning, we still seek?
Are mushrooms stronger than a leak?
With anchovies, we might just peek,
At secrets life was too shy to speak.

Each crust a question, deep and wide,
From deep dish truths to thin slice pride.
With every bite, we find our guide,
In cheesy wisdom, we confide.

So grab a slice and take a chance,
Life's more fun with a pizza dance.
In every corner, flavors prance,
With friends to share, we laugh and glance.

## **Crusty Certainties**

In the oven of existence warm,
Crusty truths take on their form.
With sauce so red, experiences swarm,
Sticking together, life's perfect norm.

We question toppings, thick or thin,
Which one's the way that leads to win?
With garlic knots, we let love in,
Certainties melt, where dreams begin.

When pineapple's thrown, it sparks a fight,
Is it a sin, or pure delight?
Doughy debates that last all night,
In silliness, we find our right.

So when the doubts start to arise,
Just order pie, and soon you'll realize,
Truths are cheesy, don't disguise,
In every slice, the laughter flies.

## Ingredients of the Soul

With flour and water, we start our quest,
Crafting a crust that'll pass the test.
What fills our hearts? We might suggest,
Those toppings add warmth, we love the zest.

Tomatoes grilled in the sun's embrace,
Dancing flavors in a vivid race.
Each bite we take, a warm, snug place,
Food for thought, with a cheesy grace.

So when we ponder, 'What's the goal?'
Remember the joy that fills the whole.
With each ingredient, we find the soul,
Pizza's the answer to make us whole.

Together we laugh, together we eat,
Tasty connections make life so sweet.
In every slice, we find our beat,
The ingredients serve up life's true feat.

## Cheesy Choices

In a world of flavors, choices abound,
Should I go classic or new be found?
With ooey-gooey cheese, I'm spellbound,
In each delicious bite, wisdom's crowned.

The toppings pile high on this big pie,
A sprinkle of joy that's hard to deny.
With friends gathered round, let's not be shy,
Cheesy choices are a reason to try.

So deep dish dreams or a thin-crust ride,
Each choice we make, there's fun to abide.
In every slice, there's laughter inside,
With pizza in hand, let's take it in stride.

So when in doubt, just grab a slice,
With every cheesy choice, oh so nice.
Life's a buffet, so think twice,
And let your heart dance in pizza's paradise.

## Saucy Revelations

When the world spins fast, I take a slice,
With pepperoni dreams and a dash of spice.
Is it fate or just cheese that pulls me near?
A crusty compass, guiding my cheer.

In the oven's warmth, I ponder it all,
Should I share this feast or heed the call?
Life bakes its lessons, hot and profound,
In every gooey bite, insights abound.

Sometimes I wonder, what toppings are wise?
A sprinkle of laughter, or surprise in the fries?
With every creation, I find my way,
In this cheesy realm, I choose to stay.

So as I munch on my savory dish,
I dream of the toppings that grant every wish.
For folks, like slices, can twist and can turn,
But together we savor; oh, how we yearn!

## The Meaning of Toppings

What's the secret to happiness, I ask my pie,
Is it loaded with bacon or toppings piled high?
Do olives bring wisdom, or jalapeños delight?
In a pizza world, wrong feels like right.

As I ponder my crust, toppings make sense,
Each flavor a riddle, no reason to fence.
From mushroom to onion, the choices run wide,
In this saucy answer, I'm filled with pride.

A sprinkle of basil, a dash of cheese,
Are the answers to life here? Oh please!
With every bite savored, a question's release,
In the toppings of truth, I find my peace.

So let's gather 'round, each slice to explore,
With crusts and great toppings, who could want more?
For this pizza of wisdom is so rich and bright,
In savory moments, all questions take flight!

## Cheesy Contemplations

In the circle of cheese, I find my muse,
Contemplating toppings I cannot refuse.
Is it better with wine, or just a cold drink?
In the sauce of existence, we all start to think.

As I chew on my crust, profound thoughts arise,
Is it stuffed or hand-tossed that brings the surprise?
With a slice in hand, I navigate fate,
Each cheesy decision, I celebrate.

What if the dough represents dreams we chase?
Rising to heights, yet finding our place.
In each melted layer, a lesson is found,
Life's a cheesy dance, spinning round and round.

With laughter and sauce, I embrace the cheer,
As I devour my pizza, it all becomes clear.
Each bite a reminder, the key is to play,
In this funny existence, let's savor the fray!

**Crust and Cravings**

When cravings call out, I heed their wish,
A crust on the side makes my dreams swish.
Is it a simple slice or a gourmet affair?
In each tasty morsel, I have not a care.

With toppings aplenty, I turn the page,
In search of the flavors that soothe and engage.
Does pineapple sing? Or green peppers reign?
In this doughy quest, there's so much to gain.

Crusty and warm, it's more than a meal,
A gathering place, where all hearts can heal.
For every slice shared is a joy that's divine,
In the world of pizza, happiness shines.

So with every bite, I savor and grin,
This joyful pursuit is where we begin.
In the dance of the crust, life surely is fun,
For in every pizza, we're all just as one!

## Pepperoni Ponderings

When the world seems full of cheese,
And toppings make you think with ease,
Is love just like a pizza pie?
It's deep and round, and oh my, my!

With each slice savored slow,
Do friendships rise like dough in tow?
Are dreams the crust we hold so dear?
Topped with hopes, is that unclear?

**Doughy Dilemmas**

In the oven of our fate,
Is it baked or is it late?
Is each moment just a bite?
Crusty edges, is that right?

When pizza's served on friendship's plate,
Can toppings make us contemplate?
Cheesy layers, rich and bold,
What warmth in chaos, stories told!

## **Sauced Solutions**

In marinara we confide,
Saucy thoughts we cannot hide.
Are the toppings like our dreams?
Layered well, or bursting seams?

A slice of hope, a pie of fate,
Each flavor is a chance we take.
With every bite, new paths we see,
In sauce we trust, so let it be!

**A Slice of Serenity**

When choices slice like pizza crust,
Do we chew with care and trust?
Is peace the garlic on our bread?
Transforming thoughts, when fear has fled?

With every slice, our worries fade,
Stretched dough gives life its trade.
Extra cheese to soothe the mind,
A bite of joy, in crust we find!

## The Crust of Understanding

Why does the cheese melt so nice?
It holds all the secrets, so precise.
Like life's deep truths, bubbling hot,
Eaten with laughter, we give it a shot.

The crust is a base, sturdy and round,
Where all of life's flavors are found.
With each flaky slice, we ponder and chew,
Eating our questions, what else can we do?

Toppings abound, like choices we crave,
From spicy debates to sweet moments we save.
Each bite a reminder, fun and sublime,
Digging for answers, one slice at a time.

## A Pizza for the Soul

What's the meaning of pepperoni's fate?
Perhaps it's just love on a plate.
With sauce like passion, bright and red,
We feast on musings that dance in our head.

An olive for wisdom, a mushroom for fun,
Each slice a story, where all are spun.
The pizza spins round, like thoughts in our mind,
In cheesy delight, new answers we find.

We gather together, with laughter and cheer,
Sharing our slices, as friends draw near.
In each gooey bite, life lessons unfurl,
As we crunch on our crust, we embrace the whirl.

## The Toppings of Truth

Is it pineapple on pizza or pizza on pine?
Questions that linger in the back of the line.
With every topping, new flavors arise,
Like truths in disguise, to surprise and to prize.

Jalapeños sting like sharp, witty quips,
While pepper flakes offer spicy little trips.
In every decision, we pile on the zest,
And find, in the chaos, we're truly blessed.

So sprinkle on joy, and add a few laughs,
Life's tasty dilemmas become our best halves.
As we savor our slices, we boldly declare,
The toppings of truth are beyond compare!

## **Crusty Curiosity**

Curiosity baked in the oven of fate,
What does life hold? Oh, let's contemplate!
With a crust so warm, full of flaky delight,
We ponder our questions in each savory bite.

Why is the world round like a pizza pie?
Perhaps it's because it spins and can fly.
As cheese stretches out in gooey delight,
Answers emerge, deep in the night.

So come grab a slice, don't let it grow cold,
In the warmth of these flavors, new stories unfold.
The crusty curiosity keeps filling our plates,
With laughter and cheese, it's never too late!

## Recipes for Reflection

When the world feels so vast,
Grab a slice, make it fast.
Toppings stacked high, never low,
Cheese dreams help worries go.

Crusty thoughts, a golden hue,
Is it deep-dish, or just me and you?
Sauce that simmers, secrets unfold,
Every bite a story told.

Pepperoni, round and bright,
Questions fade with every bite.
What's the meaning of it all?
Just enjoy, take the call.

So raise a slice, share a cheer,
Pizza points will make it clear.
In this dough, we all unite,
Happiness is our true bite!

## Savory Sentences

In a world of toppings galore,
How do you measure love, and more?
Is it thin crust or stuffed delight?
Each slice served brings pure insight.

When does the cheese pull just right?
Shall we ponder in this night?
With each topping, a new plan,
Anchovies? Only if you can!

Gather 'round, let the laughter flow,
What's the best combo? Let's not show!
With extra sauce, we'll never fall,
Pizza wisdom, a feast for all.

Crispy edges, tales untold,
In every bite, let joy unfold.
This round table makes it clear,
Food and fun, we hold so dear!

## Navigating Noodles

In a pasta world, so twisted and bright,
Is there a map to make it right?
Fettucine dreams danced with love,
A sprinkle of cheese sent from above.

How do you twirl the perfect bite?
With garlic bread, it feels so right.
Sauce that splats, with humor loud,
In this bowl we laugh, so proud.

Linguine speaks, while spaghetti sways,
Do the noodles know better ways?
With every slurp, laughter is born,
Over the table, we cheer and scorn.

Gathered here, with forks in hand,
Pasta spins, let's take a stand.
With marinara thoughts, we unwind,
In this dish, all joy combined!

## The Great Sausage Debate

On the pizza pie, who wears the crown?
Is it sausage, or shall we drown?
What's the secret of this great taste?
In every bite, let's not waste.

With peppers tossed, a colorful show,
Does meat belong, or not so so?
A sausage slice, so bold, so grand,
Discussing toppings, hand in hand.

Hawaiian? No way! Just peppered spice,
In this round, it's always nice.
With laughter ringing through the night,
Sausage reigns, or does it bite?

From every corner, voices rise,
In this debate, we share the prize.
Let's eat together, melt away dread,
For pizza's the peace, that's what it said!

## **Tantalizing Terrains**

In a world of cheese and dough,
A slice can calm the inner woe.
Crusty corners, oh so bright,
They bring the most peculiar delight.

What's the meaning of it all?
Maybe in that cheesy ball.
Each topping tells a tale unbeknown,
Beneath the oven's heat, we've grown.

Sausage songs and veggie dreams,
Life's mysteries in melted streams.
A sprinkle of herbs, a dash of zest,
On this round pie, we jest the best.

When hunger strikes, we know the way,
Grab a slice, and make your day.
With every bite, we laugh and play,
In cheesy bliss, we find our stay.

## Pondering Over Pepperoni

What's the secret? Let's inquire,
Pepperoni circles, fuels the fire.
All roads lead to this meatly charm,
With one good bite, there's no alarm.

Is the meaning found in the sauce?
Or does it dwell in dough's soft gloss?
Layered truths on every plate,
Unravel mysteries while we sate.

For every slice, a question posed,
In garlic knots, life's truths exposed.
Can pineapple really stand the test?
In every choice, we find our jest.

With laughter shared around the pie,
We muse and ponder as slices fly.
An epic quest on cheesy waves,
In pepperoni, joy enslaves.

## **The Tapestry of Toppings**

Life, it seems, is like a pie,
With layers piled, oh me, oh my!
From mushrooms dancing to olives' sway,
In toppings' tale, we laugh and play.

Is there wisdom in the crust?
A golden edge, it's pretty just.
With every sprinkle and dash of spice,
We calculate, oh so precise.

Tomatoes sing in red delight,
While cheese dreams melt in the night.
What's the moral wrapped so tight?
Dig in deeper, take a bite!

Each slice a journey, flavors swirl,
In this pizzeria, our thoughts unfurl.
So grab a chunk, let worries cease,
For in this feast, we find our peace.

## Craving Cosmic Connection

From far and wide, we gather 'round,
A pizza planet where joy is found.
With every slice, our hearts take flight,
In the cosmos of cheese, all feels right.

Is delusion found in the thick crust?
Or are we lost in flavors we trust?
Mushrooms and meats collide and dance,
In this cheesy orbit, we take a chance.

The universe within each bite,
Saucy stars shining oh so bright.
What's the secret in peppery swirls?
In every slice, our laughter twirls.

So let's toast to olives and cheese,
Celebrate flavors that aim to please.
In this galaxy of gooey grace,
With every pie, we find our place.

## **Pepperoni Profundities**

In the oven, thoughts do rise,
Toppings swirling with surprise.
Cheese like dreams, so stretchy wide,
Flavors dance, they cannot hide.

Saucy wisdom drips and flows,
Each bite a tale, the truth it shows.
Slice it up, share with friends,
In every crisper corner, laughter bends.

Merging crust with a moonlit glance,
Doughy questions lead to dance.
What's the meaning? Pass the spice!
In every crunch, we find our slice.

Cheesy quips on pepperoni,
Deep dish dreams don't feel so phony.
Take a bite, let out a cheer,
In each morsel, joy is near.

## Crusty Adventures

Crusty roads we roam tonight,
Toppings ready, futures bright.
In the oven, questions bake,
What's the risk? What's at stake?

A slice of life, a dash of zest,
Seek the pie that's truly best.
Fold it, toss it, here's the play,
Every bite leads us astray.

Sauce-stained maps and garlic knots,
Unraveled stories in the pots.
Delivery dreams in cheesy haze,
With every slice, we mend our ways.

Pizza nights and midnight rides,
In crust we trust, our hope abides.
With laughter thick like melted cheese,
On crusty journeys, we find our peace.

## In Search of the Perfect Slice

Wandering through the pizzeria door,
What lies beneath that cheese galore?
Is it joy? Is it deep regret?
Or merely fat we can't forget?

The crust, a barrier to our dreams,
A canvas where absurdity beams.
Should I go thin, or thick as fear?
Let's order both and share a beer!

Each topping tells a story bold,
Pineapple dreams, or classic gold.
In search of wisdom in the dough,
What should we add to make it glow?

Through greasy notes and melted seams,
We ponder life and laugh in beams.
In every slice, the question swirls,
A pizza love that twirls and twirls.

## Melted Memory Lane

Down the lane where cheese dreams cling,
Pizza memories laugh and sing.
Every slice, a moment stored,
In every crust, a tale is poured.

Butter-browned in the late-night glow,
The friends we've lost, the love we sow.
From schoolyard benches to butcher shops,
In melted moments, the giggling stops.

Saucy smiles and laughter share,
Memories weave through pizza flair.
The world too big to leap alone,
Let's break bread, and make it home.

Each triangle holds a secret bright,
In the slice of time, we reunite.
Gooey goodness is our golden chain,
In every slice, love stays the same.

## The Crust Beneath Our Feet

In a world of toppings piled high,
What makes us happy? Cheese or pie?
Pepperoni dreams in the night,
With every slice, the world feels right.

Crusty secrets of the universe,
Saucy tales, they can immerse.
A triangle of wisdom to devour,
Pizza's power in every hour.

Gaze into the oven's glow,
Questions rise like dough, you know?
Do we have the slice to share?
Or thin crust woes, we must beware.

So gather 'round with friends galore,
A pie of life, let's explore.
With each bite, our laughter spreads,
In cheesy truth, our hunger's fed.

## Pizza Parlor Philosophy

What's the meaning of this sauce?
Do we toss in love or loss?
The answer's found in every crust,
A cheesy heart is a must.

Mozzarella dreams and garlic breath,
Dough-formed lives—no need for death.
Each topping's like a thought we share,
A peppered ponder, a slice of care.

Are we just slices in this game?
Or rising dough with dreams to claim?
The oven's heat brings us to glow,
Bake those questions, let them grow!

In booths where laughter echoes loud,
Philosophy feels warm and proud.
So pass the pizza, share the glee,
It's hot and fresh—just like we!

## **Flavors of Fate**

On a pizza plate, we find our way,
Is fate a slice we choose each day?
Thin crust dreams or deep dish plight,
Every topping a guiding light.

Sausage talks of strength and cheer,
While veggies whisper, 'Please come near.'
Is life a mix or just plain cheese?
Tasty options put us at ease.

Bite into fate, have no regrets,
Each flavor's lesson, no need for bets.
Olives remind us to never fear,
Toppings of joy, always near.

So sprinkle laughter on every slice,
Cheesy wisdom is oh-so-nice.
A pizza party of fate awaits,
Take a piece, don't hesitate!

## In Search of the Perfect Slice

What makes a slice the very best?
Could it be cheese, or just a jest?
Is it round like our hopes and dreams,
Or square like life's odd little schemes?

In search of crust that sings with joy,
A quest for flavor, oh what a ploy!
Each bite a journey of taste and fun,
Chasing happiness 'til the day is done.

Toppings galore, a colorful sight,
Do we really need everything tonight?
With each decision, the stakes get high,
Slicing through doubts like a pie in the sky.

So gather your buddies, don't be shy,
A search for pizza—give it a try!
In every corner, a perfect piece waits,
With laughter and love, we open the gates.

www.ingramcontent.com/pod-product-compliance
Lightning Source LLC
Chambersburg PA
CBHW051630160426
43209CB00004B/592